Teen Issues

RELATIONSHIPS

Cath Senker

Heinemann
LIBRARY

Chicago, Illinois

www.capstonepub.com
Visit our website to find out more information about Heinemann-Raintree books.

To order:
☎ Phone 800-747-4992
🖳 Visit www.capstonepub.com
   to browse our catalog and order online.

Edited by Andrew Farrow, Adam Miller, and
 Vaarunika Dharmapala
Designed by Steve Mead and Clare Webber

Originated by Capstone Global Library Ltd
Printed and bound in China by Leo Paper Products Ltd

16 15 14 13 12
10 9 8 7 6 5 4 3 2 1

Library of Congress Cataloging-in-Publication Data

Senker, Cath.

  Relationships / Cath Senker.

    p. cm.—(Teen issues)

  Includes bibliographical references and index.

  ISBN 978-1-4329-6536-5 (hb)—ISBN 978-1-4329-6541-9 (pb) 1. Interpersonal relations. 2. Friendship. I. Title.

  HM1106.S46 2013

  302—dc23   2011039239

Acknowledgments

We would like to thank the following for permission to reproduce photographs: Alamy pp. 7 (© MBI), 14 (© Fancy), 17 (© John Powell Photographer), 24 (© UpperCut Images), 33 (© GlowImages), 34 (© Radius Images), 42 (© Agencja FREE); Corbis pp. 12 (© Beau Lark), 27 (© Birgid Allig), 30 (© Leah Warkentin/Design Pics), 39 (© Ocean), 41 (© Hans Neleman), 44 (© Oliver Rossi), 47 (© Juice Images), 48 (© Tim Pannell); Getty Images pp. 9 (Purestock), 18 (Hill Street Studios/Blend Images), 21 (Image Source); Glow Images p. 10 (Chris Ryan/OJO Images), 37 (A Chederros/Onoky); Rex Features p. 29 (Olycom SPA); Shutterstock pp. 4 (© ejwhite), 6 (© Liz Van Steenburgh), 23 (© Adrian Britton).

Cover photograph of two young people laughing reproduced with permission of Getty Images (Smith Collection/Taxi). Cover photograph of a decorative heart reproduced with permission of Shutterstock (© Ladybuggy). Cover photograph of a concert ticket reproduced with permission of Shutterstock (© Nicemonkey).

The author would like to thank Shelley Holland, youth counselor (www.counseling4brighton.co.uk), for her invaluable help in writing this book.

The author would also like to acknowledge the following sources for real-life stories: pp. 4–5: Daryl Taylor and AllExperts.com; pp. 32–33: www.beingastepparent.co.uk; pp. 44–45: www.childhelp.org.

CONTENTS

Some words are shown in bold, **like this**. You can find out what they mean by looking in the glossary.

RELATIONSHIP PROBLEMS

It is normal to have disagreements in families, but constant arguments are a sign of problems in a relationship.

DARYL'S STORY: I SURVIVED RELATIONSHIP PROBLEMS

"My problems started when I was just three years old. We moved, and soon afterward, my dad ran off with my mom's best friend. Life was difficult after Dad left. Mom had to work ridiculously long hours to make ends meet, and money was always tight. Then she started to see the man whose wife had run off with Dad. We spent a lot of time with his family, but we didn't get along well.

After my first year in high school, we moved. At my new school, I was bullied because I spoke and dressed differently from the others. The other kids put my coat in the garbage and covered it with dog waste and hid my bag. They taunted me to try to make me fight. So I kept away from other students during breaks. I worked hard at school, and eventually I made some friends.

But my home life remained hard—there were daily arguments. I just used to go to my room to avoid conflict. Then I was accused of being **antisocial**! My mom's partner used to get angry with me for small things such as leaving cups in my room. He told me I was nothing and would never achieve anything. He began to get violent with me and told me I wasn't welcome in the house. The others in the family knew what was going on, but they were unable to do anything about his behavior.

Studying provided an excellent escape from my troubles at home and I made new friends. I graduated from high school with good grades. I got accepted into a good college. From now on, I would be in control of my own life. I haven't looked back since."

GOOD RELATIONSHIPS

Daniel's relationships

Family:
Mom, stepdad, younger stepbrother, dad
Mom has a brother and sister. Brother is married with three children. Sister is single.
Dad is an only child. He is remarried with one daughter.

School:
Best friends in school: Aaron, Ahmed, Freddie, and Georgia
Karolina, on whom Daniel has a crush
Adults: teachers; learning disabilities teacher (Daniel has **dyslexia**)

Daniel (age 13)

Tennis team:
Coach; friends Louis, James, and Charmaine (Daniel doesn't know it yet, but she will be his girlfriend next year)

Band:
Louis and Ahmed (from the tennis team and school), Ahmed's aunt (musician who helps out), neighbor (transports instruments in van)

We are all part of a complex network of links with different people, including our family, extended family, neighbors, and friends. Take a look at the diagram of Daniel's relationships on page 6. Can you map your relationships in a similar way?

In school, you form relationships with the adults and other students, and you come to know other people through clubs, sports, and activities. Some connections are casual—you might occasionally say "hi" to the cashier at the corner store—while others last a lifetime.

Relationships between people are important. They make us feel valued, provide support, and help us enjoy life. Even casual links matter. If you are friendly to the people you meet, you can brighten their day. Being able to get along well with different people is an essential life skill.

Relationships can provoke strong feelings. In a good relationship, you feel great. For example, you may talk openly with your boyfriend or girlfriend and feel respected and loved. Your self-confidence grows. On the other hand, bad relationships can make you feel sad. Perhaps the relationship is unequal: one person dominates the other, says nasty things, or is jealous or **possessive**. Difficult relationships make life harder. So, how can you have successful relationships?

It is good to be friendly toward people, even if you do not know them well.

Meet the challenges

Relationships can be hard at times. Perhaps you have moved and have to attend a new school. Maybe your family has changed, and you have gained a new **sibling** or a stepparent. You may even have to cope with the death of someone close to you.

In new situations, you find yourself having to adapt. Even in healthy relationships, there can be problems. A particular issue might arise that divides you from a friend, relative, boyfriend, or girlfriend. So, you then have to solve the problem. You have to work at relationships to keep them going.

Develop your relationship skills

Fortunately, everyone can learn to have good relationship skills. For starters, try to keep an open mind and do your best to ignore **stereotypes**. A stereotype is when you make an assumption about someone based on fixed ideas about the person's race, skin color, religion, culture, or abilities.

For example, it is a common stereotype in Western countries that a Muslim girl who covers her head with a head scarf belongs to a family that follows strict Islamic ways. This stereotype says that this girl must do exactly what her parents or older brothers say and has no control over her own life. However, it is wise not to judge a person by his or her clothing. The Muslim girl you see may be entirely free to make choices about her life, as are many Muslim girls and women.

THINK ABOUT THIS

Consider the different relationships you have with people, such as your friends, family, and teachers. How do they vary? Do you think they could be improved in any way?

Likewise, people with disabilities may be stereotyped as weak and regarded with pity. Despite this, your classmate in a wheelchair might be a genius at science, an excellent musician, or far more athletic than you are.

When you are taking part in a group discussion, make sure that everyone has the chance to have their say.

If you learn to avoid pre-judging people and are open to getting to know them, you will gain the skills to cope with differences and embrace them. Life would be so boring if we all dressed the same, thought the same, and engaged in similar activities. Having friends from different backgrounds with varying outlooks enriches your own life.

Communicate well

Good communication is the key to healthy relationships. Think about how to really listen when another person wants to tell you something. It helps to face the person and keep eye contact to show that you are giving your full attention. Try to get rid of distractions—for example, turn off the television. You can ask questions to gain more information. Also, you can work at picking up **nonverbal behavior** such as facial expressions. Noticing these signs can help you to understand how a person is feeling. It is also important to learn to take criticism. If someone criticizes you, try to listen to what the person says rather than arguing. Perhaps the person is right!

Sharing feelings

In addition to listening, try to share your own feelings honestly with the other person. It can be tricky to say how you feel, especially if you think it might upset someone. However, remember that working through any disagreements can make your relationships stronger.

Accept changes

No matter how successful your relationships are, they change over time, and you have to adjust to this. Sometimes they end naturally because your circumstances change. Perhaps one of you leaves your school and moves to a new area, and so you lose touch. You might drift apart from a friend as you grow up, if your interests change and you no longer enjoy the same activities. This is nothing to worry about—it is a normal part of life.

Relationships that are successful and fulfilling at one stage of your life may one day change or end.

RACHEL'S STORY: A GOOD RELATIONSHIP

"I met Sadie in preschool when we were both four years old, and we've been close friends for 10 years now. Starting school was hard for me because my family had been living in another country, but Sadie and I soon became friends. We were inseparable in school and we got together in our free time, too. I remember that we were loud and giggly when we were out and about—we were always laughing together.

We moved up to middle school together, but we were put in different classes. This didn't affect our friendship too much. We did after-school activities together, such as drama club and sleepovers, and we remained best friends just as before.

Luckily, we were able to attend the same high school. There, we widened our circle of friends, so it wasn't just the two of us anymore. We both developed different interests. Sadie is a real outdoorsy girl, who loves hiking and camping with her Scout group, while I'm much more into going shopping or to the beach with a group of friends. But we've learned to give each other space to form new friendships and pursue different pastimes without jealousy creeping in. If we experience problems such as bullying or arguments with friends, we know we can rely on each other. That's the essence of a good relationship."

What is trustworthiness?

"Trustworthy would be somebody that you can depend on. Not that you need to, but ... if I tell you this, you're not gonna go tell him or her, and you're not gonna look at me differently or something like that."

A teenage girl explains her view of trustworthiness in a relationship

FRIENDSHIPS

It is normal to be nervous on your first day of school.

Do you have a best friend or a group of friends? You may have school friends, family friends, and other friends you see when you take part in activities. Everyone can make friends, although some of us find it easier than others. Problems sometimes arise in friendships, but they can usually be solved.

What makes a successful friendship?

Good friendships are based on trust. You can open up to your friends and discuss your feelings. They support you if you have a problem. Dependable friends do not become jealous if you want to spend some time with other people or just be alone. They give each other space. Even if you have occasional arguments, you manage to overcome them with a bit of effort.

Making friends

Some people find it easy to make friends because they are outgoing and happy to talk to people they have never met before. Others are shy and find it much harder. Sometimes you have no choice about making new friends—for instance, when you move or start at a different school. It helps to seem confident, even if you do not feel it! Remember that everyone has the potential to be someone's friend. You do not need to be brilliant or fascinating, and there are skills you can learn to help you.

Online friends

When you are online, be careful about who you agree to accept into your forums or private chat rooms. There are large numbers of young people using these sites, but adults with bad intentions also use them to make contact with teenagers. It is safest to be friends online only with people you know in the real world. If you do meet people online, be careful not to share your personal details with them. Never, ever go to meet anyone you have met online without a trusted adult, such as a relative or family friend.

Know yourself

It helps to know yourself and your positive traits. If you like yourself, others are more likely to like you, too! Think about your character. Are you more comfortable one-on-one or in a group? What activities do you enjoy? Friendships are often based on common interests, so think about joining a club where you will meet like-minded people.

Keeping your friends

It is important to treat your friends with respect and not to take them for granted. Try not to be bossy, but also avoid being a sheep. It is possible to strike a balance between telling others what to do and just following the crowd. If you disagree about an issue, see if you can be flexible and come to a **compromise** that everyone accepts. Sometimes tensions can arise within friendships. People who are supposed to be friends might **exclude** you or talk behind your back. If this happens, talk to them about the problem. If they are real friends, they will decide to stop doing this, or they will explain if there has been a misunderstanding.

It is a horrible feeling when you suspect that your friends are talking about you behind your back.

Peer pressure

Have you ever experienced **peer pressure**? This is pressure that comes from people of the same age in your social circle. Your friends' influence can be positive—for example, they might encourage you to succeed in a sport. Their influence can also be negative, such as when friends persuade others to take part in behavior that can get them into trouble or cause them harm. For instance, in eighth grade, Ashley's friend pushed her to stop eating: "She would tell me that I looked like a hippo in my clothes and that I needed to lose a lot of weight because I was fat. She would try to get me to starve myself." If you are put under pressure like this, trust your instincts and do not agree to do things you feel are wrong. Talk to a trusted adult. If your friends are putting negative pressure on you, it might be time to make some new friends.

Tips for making friends

- *Be open*: In a new situation, be open to friendships with different kinds of people. The more people you get to know, the more likely it is you will find people to be friends with.

- *Listen*: Rather than judging people on how they look, try to listen to what they say. You might find shared interests.

- *Smile!*: Smiling shows you are **sociable** and willing to talk.

- *Start the conversation*: Say hello and introduce yourself as confidently as you can.

- *Ask questions*: This shows that you are interested in the other person. Listen carefully and ask open questions that cannot be answered just with "yes" or "no." Open questions lead more naturally to a conversation. Remember to make eye contact from time to time, to show you are giving the other person your full attention. (Do not stare at someone—that will make the person nervous!)

- *Be complimentary*: Pay the person a compliment and then tag on a question to get a conversation going.

Surviving arguments

Even in healthy relationships without jealousy, arguments can flare up. Arguments can differ for boys and girls. Girls tend to have intense friendships. If someone says something mean, they can get extremely upset, and the feeling lasts. Boys are more likely to have an argument or a fight, but then it is all over. Major disagreements may need to be sorted out, though. It is wise to wait until you have both calmed down, and then discuss the problem. Try to listen to criticism, and if you were in the wrong, say you are sorry! If you are not to blame, it is fine to stand up for yourself. Maybe another friend or neutral person could talk to both of you and help you to reach an agreement. If you have different opinions, you may need to agree to disagree, or compromise. It may take time for your relationship to get back to normal after the argument and you may feel a little insecure, but that is natural.

Ending a friendship

In extreme cases, an argument might end a friendship, but sometimes the relationship fades naturally. People might drift apart because they no longer have much in common. This is particularly hard if just one of you wants to end the friendship. If you would like to stop being friends, try the gentle approach. You could stop getting in touch, or if your friend invites you over, say you have other plans. Some people will understand, but not all. If someone does not get the message, it is best to be honest and say as kindly as possible that you want to end the friendship.

If you are at the receiving end of this treatment, it does not mean there is something wrong with you. Just try to accept that people can grow apart over time. Focus on new interests and getting to know other people. Later on, you might reflect that breaking off the friendship marked the end of one phase of your life and the start of a fresh one.

TRUE OR FALSE?

Boys can be emotional as well as girls

True. In most modern societies, boys are expected to be tough and not to show emotions or cry. However, boys as well as girls need to be able to talk about their feelings and express their emotions.

Jealousy

Jealousy comes from feelings of insecurity. You might envy your best friend because you believe he is better looking than you. Perhaps he is jealous of *you*. A little jealousy is natural, but try not to let it affect your behavior. Rather than comparing yourself with others, try to focus on your own aims and good qualities.

Jealousy can lead to bullying. A group of young people may target a student for doing well in school because they are envious. Bullying should never be tolerated. If someone acts jealously toward you, try to avoid the person. Always consult a trusted adult if the situation is causing you stress.

Boys tend to be more likely than girls to engage in physical bullying.

If you join a club in school, you will meet people who share your interests and passions.

In school, you do not choose the other students or the teachers, but you have to get along with them! Close friendships are often formed in school, since you spend a lot of time together. Yet there can be challenges if you switch to a new school or are bullied by an unfriendly group. These difficulties can be overcome, though.

You may be lucky and start a new school with some friends. Otherwise, you will need to make the effort to get to know people. Do not forget that most other people will be in the same position. It should be easy enough to form relationships with your classmates, even if you just work together in class. To meet other people with similar interests, find the courage to join a club at school. Do not worry if no one you know is going along. You will soon make new friends.

New school, new friends

Have you ever started at a new school halfway through the year? When everybody already knows each other, finding friends can seem impossible. You just need to be patient. Start by talking to one person, and once you know that person, you can begin chatting to his or her friends.

Whenever a new classmate joins your class, do your best to be friendly. Imagine how you would feel if it were you! Smile and talk to the person. Even if you do not become friends, the person will appreciate your efforts to be welcoming in the first weeks. The same applies if you notice someone being left out or bullied by his or her usual friends. Invite the person to hang out with you, at least until he or she sorts out any problems.

THINK ABOUT THIS

People in school often have a circle of friends. They may also have contact with many more friends through Facebook or other social networking sites. Such sites are great for staying in touch with friends and arranging your social life. Remember, though, that genuine friendships involve trust. You may have hundreds of online "friends" whom you do not know very well. Is it possible to have too many friends? Also, think about the kinds of pictures and comments that people post on social networking sites. Would some of them be better shared with a small group of genuine, trusted friends, rather than sent out to a large group?

Feeling left out

"I recently switched schools from a public school to an all-girls private school; I'm 14 years old. I have friends ... at my new school, we all get along great and I enjoy hanging out with them. But they mostly live close to each other, while I live a little farther away.

Lots of other girls my age are meeting up with their close friends every weekend, having sleepovers, shopping, doing lots of stuff together ... I would love to see some of my friends outside school, but I feel I'm not close enough to them to ask them."

Mia, age 14

Friendship frictions

Bullying people and excluding them are common issues at school. If you have a disagreement with your friends and they are excluding you, share your feelings with someone—a classmate, teacher, or another trusted adult. If your former friends are bullying you, you should definitely tell a teacher. While you are sorting out the bullying, take time to identify other people you could befriend and try approaching them.

Even if you do have good school friends, you might feel left out when they meet up in their free time. Perhaps they do not ask you because you do not live nearby or your parents are strict about allowing you to go out. Gather the courage to ask them to meet up somewhere you can all reach easily or invite them to your house.

Relating to teachers

You probably have a favorite teacher whose classes are fun, plus you enjoy the subject. Others teachers you may not like at all. Yet you will learn better if you treat them with respect and attempt to get along with them all.

It can be hard to approach a group of people who are already friends. Instead, you can try meeting people one at a time.

SARAH'S STORY: LEAVING A CLIQUE

Sarah's story begins in preschool, where she became friends with nine little girls. The 10 soon became a **clique**. By middle school, the clique had become more like a pack. The girls all dressed in the most exclusive name-brand clothing, wore their hair exactly the same way (long and straight), and laughed at other girls who could not (or would not) dress like them. The girls started calling themselves the Top 10.

Using a combination of exclusion and cruelty, the Top 10 **intimidated** both kids and adults … Though Sarah was a member of the Top 10, she felt trapped. She knew what she was doing was wrong, but she did not have the courage to confront her friends about their bullying or to leave the relative safety of the group … Sarah begged her parents to let her switch schools … Moving to a new school would make many teenagers miserable, but Sarah was relieved.

Cliques: The pros and cons

A common way to ensure you are not left out at school is to be part of a clique, a group of friends who spend their time together. Cliques can be a lot of fun. You are never alone, and you feel secure and wanted.

Most cliques are simply groups of people who share an interest, such as skateboarding, music, or computer games. However, some cliques are more like gangs. Gangs are generally groups of young people who encourage each other to do antisocial, dangerous, or illegal things. (To find out more, read the *Gangs* book in this series.)

Members of this type of clique sometimes turn nasty when they are together. Often, one or two dominant people decide who can join the clique and who will be left out. It may be based on how they look, what they wear, or their activities. The **group dynamics** can encourage people to be hostile to others. It is easier to pick on people if you are in a group than on your own. The clique may pick on outsiders or on people they no longer want in the group.

Surviving a clique

If you are in a clique, make sure that you can be yourself, too. You should never have to change your behavior to suit others. Try not to take part in ganging up on someone who has fallen out of favor with the group. Think about how miserable it is to be left out—it could be you, too, one day! People who experience this feel lonely and isolated, and their **self-esteem** is damaged.

If your clique is bullying others, try to persuade your friends to stop. If you cannot, you could decide to leave the clique. Then you can choose your friends, and no one will tell you to dress or act in a certain way.

A close group of friends can be great, as long as they are not cruel to others.

ATTRACTION AND DATING

These people look a little embarrassed. Perhaps they have a crush on each other!

Have you ever felt attracted to anyone? Perhaps you have had a crush on someone you know at school. Perhaps you really like somebody you do not know, such as a movie star or sports personality. Maybe you have already started dating. Just like any relations between people, you need to work at dating relationships. In the best relationships, you and your partner go at your own pace and never feel pressured into doing anything you do not want to.

What is attraction?

People find others attractive for various reasons, such as how they look or speak, or their personality. Usually, we first notice how someone looks. Sometimes attraction is instant, while at other times it takes a while to develop. You can be attracted to a person as a friend or experience romantic attraction.

Crushes

A crush is when you have strong feelings about someone, even if you barely know the person. It could be a celebrity from television or a movie, a teacher, or another student. If it is a celebrity, you do not really know what the person is like. On the other hand, if you develop intense feelings toward a boy or girl you know, it may feel quite embarrassing when you see your crush. You might blush or be tongue-tied and not know what to say around the person. You might be incredibly nervous when you are near the person. This is perfectly normal.

A fantasy world

"It was my chemistry teacher … I liked her a lot and at some point my emotions and hormones mixed. It was all in the fantasy world I created in my daydreams; in real life I was the same helpful, studious boy for her."

A man recalls a crush he had at the age of 14

Coping with a crush

When you have a crush, you might find it hard to concentrate in school or even to eat or sleep, because you are so obsessed with the person. You cannot stop thinking about the person. It is fine to allow yourself some time for fantasies about your crush, but try not to let your obsession take over your entire life. It may help to confess to your friends and allow them to distract you. Try to keep up your normal activities or even find a new hobby to focus on.

Asking someone out

So, how can you turn a crush into a date? Of course, it will really only be possible if it is a young person you already vaguely know. First, you will need to get to know the person. When you meet, try to get into a conversation and show that you are interested in the other person (see the tips on page 15). Try to stay relaxed. If the conversation goes well, you could ask if the person would like to exchange numbers, so that perhaps you could meet again. It is best not to be too pushy, though.

Not dating?

Young people often feel pressure to have a boyfriend or girlfriend, but do not worry if you do not have one. It will happen in time. There is no point in going out with someone just for the sake of it.

If your crush is eager to meet you again, then it sounds as if he or she is interested. Even so, it is best not to rush into things. The key is to become friends—be yourself and try to act naturally, so that you feel comfortable together. Once you have gotten to know each other, then you could suggest going out—for example, for a coffee or to the movies. It is a good idea to avoid a direct question such as, "Will you go out with me?" If the other person shares your feelings, he or she will be pleased and will happily accept your invitation to go out, and if not, then at least you will have made a friend.

Asking people out is stressful, but talking to a good friend about it can help.

Dealing with rejection

So, what do you do if your crush is not interested? Some crushes are unrealistic in the first place. It might be quite exciting to have a crush on a celebrity or a teacher and talk about what it would be like to have a date with him or her. Yet you know it is not really going to happen. If you have a crush on someone whom you know, and that person is not interested in you, it can be extremely upsetting. Try to remember that it does not mean there is something wrong with you. Perhaps that person is not right for you or is uninterested in dating at the moment. It may not feel like it when it happens, but in time you will get over it.

First date!

You will probably be nervous about your first date, but there are ways to cope. Remember that your date will probably be nervous, too! It might be a good idea to meet in a park or café, so if the conversation is hard work, you can leave after an hour. If you choose the movies, you can talk about the movie afterward. In either case, try to think of a few topics of conversation beforehand to avoid any embarrassing silences.

First kiss

Young people may worry about kissing on a date, but there are no rules about this. It might happen when you have been dating for just a short time or when you have gotten to know each other better. Every couple is different. Kissing can happen quite naturally when you are both relaxed and enjoying yourselves. How do you know when the time is right? It is best to check the other person's reactions for clues. Make eye contact with them and judge their body language. If they do not seem to respond to you, it would be wise to wait for another opportunity.

Sex

If a relationship becomes serious, one or both of the partners may want to start having sex. It is important that no one is rushed into this decision. Remember that it is wrong for a person to be pressured into having sex, no matter what age or gender they are. It is also important that, before making this decision, people are aware of all the issues and choices involved. They may be influenced by many factors, including their personal beliefs, religious background, or concerns about pregnancy and disease.

Safe sex and abstinence

Safe sex is about avoiding becoming pregnant or catching **sexually transmitted diseases (STDs)**. It is possible to become pregnant or catch a disease the very first time a person has unprotected sex. The safest sex is always no sex! This practise is called abstinence. If a person is having sex, however, the best way for them to protect themselves and their partner from STDs and pregnancy is to use a condom.

It is a good idea to talk to your partner about sex, even though you might find it embarrassing. One way to raise the subject might be to talk about your personal beliefs or about **contraception**. If you are not able to talk about sex with your partner, this may mean you are not yet ready.

Each country has laws about the age at which you can legally have sex. In the United States, it is legal for you to consent to have sex between the ages of 16 and 18. This varies by state. Attitudes in society toward sex vary widely, from those who believe that people should not have sexual relations until they are married, to others who think people should be able to have sex freely as long as both parties consent to it.

Falling in love

It is difficult to define love. You may have an intense crush and be obsessed with the other person; this is called **infatuation**. Love is deeper than this. It involves caring about the other person's well-being, sharing the person's problems, and being committed to the person during bad times as well as happy times.

In our culture, media images encourage young people to look and act sexy.

29

Overcoming problems

Many issues that crop up between a couple can be solved by good communication. A girl might feel possessive about her boyfriend and always want to know what he is doing. A boy may be jealous of the time his girlfriend spends with her friends. If there is something that is bothering you, then bring it out in the open. Jealous partners may just be feeling insecure and just want a bit of reassurance.

They're prejudiced!

"My Chinese-American boyfriend and I have been dating for six months. His parents are happy that he is dating me and have no problem with me. This is totally different with my parents! They cannot understand why I don't want a white man, but prefer an Asian one ... My parents are very prejudiced against any other ethnicities except our own."

A young woman describes her parents' prejudice

A couple from different racial backgrounds may experience prejudice.

Coping with prejudice

Occasionally, other people may come between a couple. For example, you may experience **prejudice** if you come from different racial or religious backgrounds. One or both of the families may disapprove of the relationship for these reasons, or because they do not like your partner's appearance or social class. Perhaps your parents do not approve of the person's family. They may make it clear that they dislike your partner by being unfriendly when he or she visits.

Try to discuss the issue with your parents, or if this really is not possible, then with another relative or family friend. Prejudice often arises from ignorance about the other person. You could look for a way for your boyfriend or girlfriend and parents to get to know each other. For example, they might share a common interest.

Changing feelings

Over time, two people may drift apart, just as friends can (see page 10). One person may no longer be interested in the other person, or he or she might meet someone else and be more attracted to this new person. Many young people decide they are not ready to commit to one person, which is perfectly reasonable. If the relationship is not working out, it is better to be honest about how you feel and end it. Be sensitive to the other person and tell him or her face-to-face, if possible. Avoid cowardly options such as simply sending a text!

TRUE OR FALSE?

If your friend goes out with someone you like, the friendship will have to end.

False! However, this situation is a really big test of friendship. If you are very close, you may feel that the friendship is too important to lose. Perhaps you can come to terms with what has happened, although it may take some time.

Staying safe on a date

There is no need to be overly scared about going out on a date, but you can take sensible precautions to keep safe. When you arrange a date, tell a parent or guardian where you are going and when you will be back. If you do not yet know your date well, try to meet in a public place during the daytime. Then, if for any reason you feel uncomfortable, it will be easy to leave.

Deciding to meet somewhere in public shows your date that you are not yet ready to be intimate. If you opt to spend the time alone at your home or your date's home, this might indicate that you are interested in sexual activity. Make sure that you do not give out the wrong signals!

Try to summon up the confidence to communicate what is right for you. If a date starts to touch you and you do not feel happy about it, it is best to explain that you are not ready for intimacy yet. Try to say this as sensitively as possible, so you do not hurt the other person's feelings.

Sometimes young people are pressured into behavior they are uncomfortable with. One girl described how she was drawn into having sex: "My boyfriend wants me to do sex things with him but the only way I can manage is when I get drunk because otherwise I am too scared or embarrassed." It appears this girl is not ready to have sex or is with the wrong person. She is masking the difficulties by using alcohol. The relationship is not good for her, and she is being placed in a very unfair situation.

Avoiding trouble

No matter how careful you are, you could end up in a situation in which you are frightened that you will be **sexually assaulted**. What should you do? Try to talk your way out of the situation. Stay calm and try to breathe out slowly to relax. Avoid becoming aggressive and talk quietly and clearly. Make it clear that "no means no." Hopefully, you will be able to avoid confrontation, but if you sense that the other person is not listening to reason, run away. If you are trapped and cannot escape, scream and shout out a clear instruction for passersby—for example, "Call the police!"

Drinking dangers

Alcohol dulls your senses and makes you less aware of what is going on. It is also illegal for minors to drink. Alcohol frequently leads young people to have unplanned sex, which they may later regret. If you find yourself in a situation in which your date is drinking, avoid taking part. Keep a clear head and stay safe.

Spiked drinks

It is best not to accept drinks from strangers. They may have been **spiked**. A typical drug used in this situation is Rohypnol, which causes memory loss and slows down the body's responses. Rohypnol is known as the "date rape" drug because of the ease of sexually assaulting a person who has taken it unknowingly.

These young people are having a good time without drinking alcohol.

FAMILY RELATIONSHIPS

You may have a completely different personality from your sibling, but you can still get along well.

What is your family like? You may live with both your parents and perhaps one or more siblings, or with just one parent. Maybe you live with your extended family, with a stepfamily, are adopted, or live in foster care. Family relationships can alter as you grow up or if the family changes through divorce or remarriage.

People first develop relationship skills at home. When the ties within the family are strong, people receive love and support from each other. In particular, the bond between adults in a family affects the children. If young people learn healthy relationship skills at home, then it will be easier for them to form good relations with others outside the home.

Sibling relationships matter too. Brothers and sisters usually have a special connection. Their shared experiences can bring them close and they can help each other. There can also be **rivalry** between siblings. It is advisable not to compare yourself with a sibling, but rather to respect your differences and focus on your own positive traits.

Everyone in the family has his or her own needs and wants, and sometimes these clash. Stress can increase at times as well—for example, if there is an illness or a death in the family or money problems. In these situations, the family members need to try to be open about the problems and talk to each other to resolve the issues.

Tips for handling sibling rivalry

- Ignore the insults—just walk away.
- Take 10 deep breaths to calm down before you say or do anything.
- Give your sibling space. Each day, spend some time away from each other.
- If you cannot solve a problem between you, go to a parent.
- Know that it is normal to argue with a sibling, and appreciate the good times.

Parents: What do they do for you?

Many young people believe their parents control their lives. On the other hand, parents often think their children are ungrateful for all they do for them. Clashes between parents and young people commonly occur. Why does this relationship become strained?

During the teenage years, you are becoming more independent and probably want to spend less time with your family. Yet your parents still take responsibility for you—they may offer a home, food, clothes, money, and practical and emotional support. They might help you with homework, pay for your activities, and take you on vacations. Consider the situation from your parents' point of view. They have to start allowing you some independence, but they want to ensure that you focus on your education. Parents also worry about harmful life choices, such as smoking, because they are concerned for your safety.

Rules

Parents often make rules to keep you safe. They may restrict the places you are permitted to go or insist you are home by a certain time. There may also be rules for sharing chores around the house. Rules vary widely from family to family. If you are unhappy about a rule in your home, then try to discuss it to see if it could be changed.

Some young people complain that their parents impose harsh rules. People from different backgrounds, cultures, and religious traditions have varying expectations of their children. For instance, some parents may already have an idea of what they want their children to be when they grow up and put pressure on them to do well in certain areas—even though it is not the young person's choice.

Other parents may insist on a strict code of behavior. For example, they might not allow their teenage children to date, even though others their age do. Try to appreciate their position and see if it is possible to come to a compromise.

THINK ABOUT THIS

Should parents have more say because they are adults and have more experience than you? Or should everyone's opinion count equally?

Tips for negotiating with parents:

- Stay calm—do not shout!
- Try to understand your parents' point of view.
- Explain your opinions in a **constructive** way.
- Try to reach a compromise.
- Do something in return.
- Stick to your agreement.
- Be patient. It may take time to negotiate a change.

It might help to share an activity with your parents and use the time to talk to them about what is bothering you.

Coping with a family breakup

Many young people have to deal with their parents splitting up. If this happens, you may experience a variety of feelings. For example, you may feel guilty. However, it is *not* your fault. It only involves the adults. You may be angry with them or anxious about changes to your life, such as having to move. Whatever the situation is, remember that both your parents still love you.

New scenarios

Even if it is upsetting at the time, separation can be positive. At best, the parents part on friendly terms. They may communicate clearly with everyone in the family and involve the children in decisions that affect them, such as where they are going to live. A separation is not always bad for young people. It can be better than living with parents who are enduring the stress of a relationship that has gone wrong.

At worst, there could be a period when the parents are still arguing over money, property, and the children. If just one partner wanted the separation, the other might be more upset, and you could find yourself supporting that parent. One parent might be particularly bitter and try to use the children to check up on the other parent or expect them to handle all the communications. It is unfair for a parent to use you in a fight against your other parent. Try to explain carefully that you would prefer not to discuss either of them with the other person.

If the situation is awkward, you may need support yourself. You might need to talk to your parents or a sibling to try to understand what is happening. If your emotions are overwhelming you, creative activities can be a useful outlet. You could choose to write about your feelings in a diary. Alternatively, you might like to take part in activities such as music or sports to take your mind off things. If you are finding it hard to cope, you could also seek professional help from a **counselor** or help line.

Relationships in a one-parent family

After a breakup or the death of a parent, you might find yourself living in a single-parent family. What might that be like? Daily life could become harder because of money problems. You might need to take on more responsibilities to help your parent, and he or she might share worries and ask you for advice. Perhaps your parent will treat you more like an adult and you will develop a closer bond. It will take time for your relationship to adjust.

A go-between

One 16-year-old girl reported, "Mom and Dad split up. Since then, I feel like they've used me as a go-between in their arguments. Mom and Dad don't speak to each other and I am expected to pass messages."

Parents acting like teenagers!

Single parents may start behaving differently—going out more, buying fashionable clothes, and dating new people. They may meet someone special, and you will have to get to know this person. This may go smoothly, but if you feel you are being neglected or your parent's behavior is annoying you, then discuss it when you are alone together.

It can be hard to talk about a tricky problem with a parent, but it is better to speak out than to bottle up feelings.

Accepting a stepfamily

If your parent remarries, the situation can be awkward at first. Remember that one parent's remarriage may be painful for your other parent, especially if the marriage ended because of an affair, and the ex is marrying the new partner. Try to be sensitive to this when you spend time together.

TRUE OR FALSE?

You can never be as close to a step-relative as to a blood relative.

False. A stepparent can never replace a child's **biological parent**, but the two can still become very close over time. Stepbrothers and sisters can also develop close bonds with each other.

It can be difficult for you to accept your parent's new partner. It may feel as if he or she is trying to take the place of your other parent. Your stepparent may bring in new rules or try to influence your behavior. Stepparents may bring their own children to live with you, so there will be a period of adjustment while you get used to each other. Whether you like them or not, you will need to live in the same house. Also, you may feel that your stepparent treats you differently from his or her own children. Then a new baby may come along, bringing yet another relationship into the mix.

Whenever you have concerns, it is best to talk to your parent about how your stepparent treats you. Remember that it is tricky for the stepparent, too, so try to understand his or her point of view. It will take time for everyone to adjust to the situation and become comfortable with each other. However, stepfamilies can be very happy. As Daniel says, "At the time it was tough. The breakup of my parents' marriage was bad news. Then I came to accept it, and the remarriage of my dad. Gradually the relationship has grown, and I now see my stepmom as a blessing."

LUKE'S STORY: I GAINED A STEPFAMILY

"When my parents split up, things were fairly straightforward. I went to live with my dad, and he gave me plenty of attention. Then on the weekends I saw my mom, and we spent time together. I had the best of both worlds.

Then Dad met Lisa, and they started going out. When I was 14, Lisa became my stepmom and she moved in with us, along with her 11-year-old daughter, Jennie. Lisa was nice to me— I liked her and we got along well. But I didn't feel the same way about Jennie. I thought she was spoiled and got away with things that I wouldn't have gotten away with. Perhaps it was because she was a girl and was only 11, but to me, it seemed like Lisa favored her daughter and gave her special treatment. Anyway, I wasn't used to having females around, and it felt like the pair of them had taken over our house.

Gradually, the relationships between us improved and we get along fine. We even go on vacation together. My mom gets along well with Lisa, Dad, and Jennie, so we've become one big family. But it took a lot of effort to work things out and it took a long time."

It can take time to get used to living in a bigger family, but it can be fun.

WHEN RELATIONSHIPS GO BAD

In the long run, it is better to deal with a conflict as soon as possible. Having a face-to-face conversation is a good way to go about it.

It is a sad fact of life that relationships can go horribly wrong. Young people may suffer bullying, **abuse**, or the death of someone close. No matter how **traumatic** the events, people can survive the pain caused by the experience, and good relationships can be built up afterward.

Coping with conflict

If you have a conflict with somebody, it is best to deal with it. Otherwise it can cause bitterness and damage the relationship even more. Try to negotiate with the other person. Listen to the person's viewpoint to understand how he or she feels. Then express your opinion calmly. Be assertive and make your feelings known, without being aggressive or becoming angry. It is important to respect the other person. Once you have exchanged views, see if you can find a solution that you can both accept. If you succeed in solving the conflict, your relationship may become stronger.

Tackling bullying

Bullying is hurting others using words or physical violence or by excluding them. Bullying could be face-to-face or **cyberbullying** online. (To find out more, read the *Bullying* book in this series.) If people become bullies, the problem lies with them. Perhaps they feel jealous of someone and want to take revenge, or they have low self-esteem and bully others to make them feel more powerful. If you are bullied, seek help to stop it (see page 15).

My mom drinks and bullies me

"I am being hit by my mom, who drinks a lot. She is always yelling at me, even if I haven't done anything wrong."

Boy, age 11

The agony of abuse

Abuse is the cruel treatment of another person, and it indicates serious relationship problems. It may be physical, such as hitting someone, or it may be emotional. Emotional abuse is hurting somebody's feelings by making fun of the person or continually hurling insults. **Sexual abuse** is forcing a person to take part in sexual activity. In some circumstances, it is known as rape. The abuser is often a relative or someone else who knows the victim well.

Why does it happen? Some people cannot manage their feelings properly or they have a mental illness. Alcohol is frequently a trigger. As Dave, 16, says, "My dad's great most of the time, but he gets really violent when he drinks."

Abuse is extremely frightening for the victim. If the abuser is close to a young person and is supposed to care for him or her, the behavior is also confusing. Abusers may say that they are treating people in this way because they love them. The abuse may continue for a long time and even begin to seem normal to the person who endures it.

However, abuse has no place in a healthy relationship. It can have a dramatic effect on the victims, who may lose their self-esteem, find it hard to trust others, and experience great loneliness.

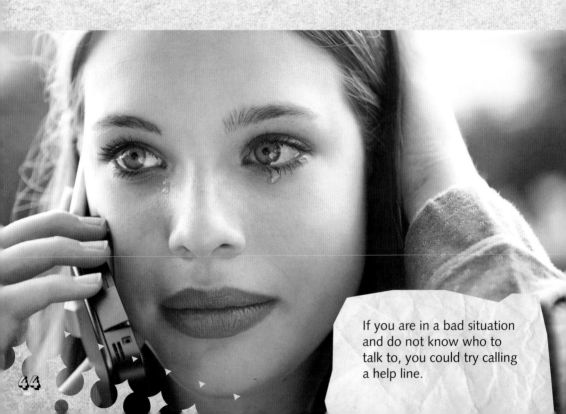

If you are in a bad situation and do not know who to talk to, you could try calling a help line.

LYDIA'S STORY: I SURVIVED ABUSE

"I was 17 years old. I remember standing at the front door, terrified. I knew ... what was going to happen. I took a deep breath and opened the door.

My alcoholic father was waiting for me. He grabbed me by the hair and started to beat me over and over again with his belt. Then he threw me against the patio door. I heard screaming behind me, as my knees buckled and I went limp. It was Mom. Dad grabbed her and threw her to the floor as well. She got up and continued to scream, "Stop! You're going to kill her!"

Eventually, Mom got him to stop beating me, and I was told to go to my room. I went to the bathroom, took off my shirt, and examined my back in the mirror. There were deep red marks from the belt all over, and some were bleeding. I cleaned myself up; the cuts were stinging. I went to my room and could hear my parents shouting in the living room.

I was so distraught that I was thinking of killing myself. Instead, I called a child help line and the woman on the phone helped me through that terrible night. She spoke to me kindly and let me talk. I will always be grateful to her. Later, I had **counseling** and the pain lessened, although I will always bear the emotional scars from the abuse."

Lydia's story shows that even in the worst situations, there are people who can help.

TRUE OR FALSE?

People who were abused will later abuse others.

False. While many people who abuse others suffered from it themselves, this does not mean that all victims will become abusers.

Speaking up about abuse

If young people are victims of abuse, they may feel ashamed because of the horrible things that have been done to them or somehow feel that they are responsible. However, it is not their fault. Their abusers might have told them that the abuse should remain a secret, or threatened to harm them if they tell someone. No matter how scared a young person is, it is better to speak up.

Abuse is never right, and it is against the law. Find a trusted adult to help stop the abuse. If the abuser is a relative, it may be difficult to tell a family member. In this case, it is better to speak with a teacher, school counselor, or a help line. Nobody should suffer alone or in silence.

What if your parent is a victim?

If a parent is being abused, it can be hard to understand why he or she puts up with the situation. A parent may be frightened to leave because he or she has no money and nowhere else to go. People who have been abused over a long period may feel too beaten down to act. Abusers can be extremely skilled at persuading their victims to stay.

If you discover your parent is being abused, talk to him or her. Your parent may not realize that you know about it. Ask your parent to seek help. If the parent is unwilling, speak to someone you trust, such as an adult friend, a teacher, or a doctor. You could also call a help line (see page 55 for organizations to contact). If you witness your parent suffering from violence, do not try to intervene—you may get hurt yourself.

The trauma of illness or death

Other traumatic relationship issues involve the serious illness or death of a friend or family member. It is a strain supporting and caring for a loved one who is gravely ill. If the person dies, you might experience a range of reactions, from shock, sadness, and anger to relief at the ending of the person's pain or complete numbness.

If you are coping with illness or loss, it is essential to express your emotions. You may prefer to work through the feelings alone, through creative activities such as writing or music, or to talk with friends or relatives or a professional counselor. Perhaps you feel more comfortable talking **anonymously** using an online or phone help line. If a loved one has died, be patient. It can take a long time to come to terms with the loss and learn to live your life without the person.

A little help from your friends

"When my younger sister, Bethany, was diagnosed with cancer, it was important for the family to support each other. I'm normally the quiet one of the family and am shy. At first, it took me a while just to talk to anyone about it ... Tell people like your close friends, so they can help you out and give you advice if you're stressed out."

Sean, age 13

Make sure you take care of yourself and plan some outings or take part in sports or exercise to keep physically active, which will help your mental state.

WHAT HAVE WE LEARNED?

Everyone, whether they are young or old, needs to work at keeping their relationships healthy.

Be yourself!

To have healthy relationships, you need to know and appreciate yourself. Think about your personality and what you are like:

- Are you shy or outgoing?
- Do you love big groups or prefer one-on-one time?
- Do you love the outdoors or do you prefer indoor activities?

Remember, there are no right or wrong answers. Differences are what make life interesting!

We have explored a variety of relationships and how important they are to our happiness. We have examined how relationships change over time, becoming closer or more distant—or ending altogether. We have also looked at ways to meet new people and how to build and maintain successful relationships.

How to have good relationships

Healthy relationships involve trust and honesty and people's willingness to help each other during the good times and the bad. In a successful relationship, neither person expresses jealousy nor restricts the other person. Both are free to follow their own interests in addition to being committed to the relationship.

You can develop your relationship skills by being open-minded and not judging people before you know them. You can learn to set **boundaries** to make sure you are treated well and prevent others from taking advantage of you. For example, you might ask your friends not to text you late at night. Say "no" when you need to and stick to doing what feels right for you!

In relationships, it is essential to be able to communicate well—to express your feelings and listen to others. If you understand each other's point of view, you can figure out the solution to any problems together. You may need to come to a compromise. During the teenage years, young people often clash with parents and need to find a way to negotiate with them.

Dealing with change and moving on

Sometimes relationships end because one or both of the parties want it to finish or their circumstances have changed. This is natural. If one person wants to end the relationship, he or she should do so as sensitively as possible. However, in bad relationships, it may not be practical to solve the problems yourself. If there are serious issues, such as bullying or abuse, it is a good idea to ask a trusted adult for help.

Young people may experience the breakup of their parents' relationship and the challenge of moving and adapting to living with new family members. As in all relationships, good communication can help to smooth the process. This is the key to successful relationships: do not bottle up your feelings, but be open and honest. Other people will respect you for it!

RESEARCH AND DEBATE

You can find out more about relationships from a variety of sources. Think about whether your source is reliable and consider the perspective of the person who produced it. Might the person be trying to promote a particular point of view?

Books

Nonfiction books and pamphlets written for young people are an excellent source of accurate and accessible information. Written by professional writers and checked by experts, the materials have been designed especially for young readers and provide a balanced view of the topic, backed up by evidence. Check the publication date of the book and try to find the most up-to-date titles. At the back of the book, you will usually find a useful list of additional resources, such as web sites and organizations to contact.

Web sites

Web sites run by highly respected, established organizations, such as mental-health organizations, are excellent sources of trustworthy information (see pages 54–55). They usually have case studies and quotes, so you can find firsthand information about other people's experiences.

Firsthand information is also available from surveys about various issues. Organizations working with young people often publish the results of their research online. Check that the source is recent, to ensure the information is up-to-date.

A warning about sources

Not all web sites are helpful or reliable. Anyone can set up a web site or blog and write what they like; no one checks if it is true or not. Beware of sites that are run by individuals and express their point of view alone.

Chat rooms can be a great way to interact with others who have shared similar experiences. Speaking with other young people can help you feel supported. However, it is extremely important to use chat rooms with caution.

Since chat sessions are "live," users may say things that are inappropriate or even hurtful. Also, some young people you meet there might not even actually be young. They could be adults who want to hurt young people. Make sure you never reveal personal information, such as your name or address, and never agree to meet anyone from a chat room in person.

Organize your research materials

If you are researching relationships for a school project, start by organizing your research materials into different categories. You could use the concept web in this book as a starting point:

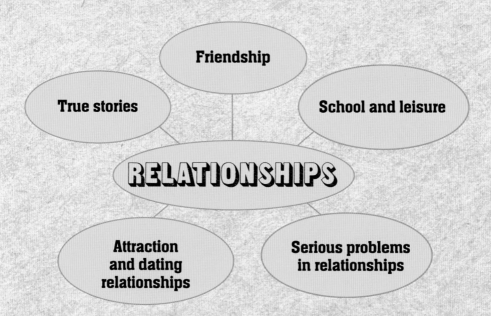

Using information for discussion and debate

If you are planning a discussion about relationships, remember that it can be an extremely sensitive topic. Remember that in a class of 30 students, there are certain to be some who are currently experiencing all sorts of difficulties in their own relationships. You may want to use role-playing in your debate. Different groups could adopt a different perspective and argue from that point of view. You could use the topics in the "Think about this" boxes in this book as discussion points.

GLOSSARY

abuse treat someone violently or cruelly. Abuse can be physical or emotional.

anonymous having an unknown identity

antisocial not wanting to spend time with other people. It can also mean acting in a way that is harmful or annoying to other people.

biological parent natural rather than an adoptive parent

boundaries limits of what is and is not acceptable behavior. This applies to how you treat others as well as how others treat you. Setting boundaries helps make sure you are treated well and prevents people from taking advantage of you.

clique small group of people who spend their time together and do not allow others to join them

compromise agreement made between two people in which each side gives up something so that both sides accept the situation

constructive helpful or useful

contraception methods of preventing pregnancy. Some of these methods include the birth control pill and condoms.

counseling professional advice about a problem

counselor person who has been trained to advise people with problems, especially personal problems

cyberbullying using electronic technology, such as e-mail, instant messaging, web sites, or texts, to bully someone

dyslexia condition involving difficulty learning to read or interpret words, letters, and other symbols

exclude leave someone out

group dynamics way in which members of a group react to each other

infatuation intense but often short-lived attraction or crush

intimidate frighten or threaten someone so that he or she does what you want

nonverbal behavior not involving words or speech

peer pressure pressure to do the same things as other people around you of the same age

possessive demanding total attention and not wanting the other person to be independent

prejudice negative feelings toward a group of people that are not based on facts

rivalry when two people are competing—for example, siblings may compete for their parents' attention or affection

self-esteem feeling of being happy with your own personality, appearance, and abilities

sexual abuse when a child or young person is forced to take part in any kind of sexual activity with an adult or young person

sexual assault any unwanted sexual behavior, usually but not always violent, that causes humiliation, pain, fear, or intimidation

sexually transmitted disease (STD) any disease that is spread through sexual intercourse

sibling brother or sister

sociable happy to be around other people and take part in conversations and activities

spike add drugs or alcohol to someone's food or drink without the person being aware

stereotype idea, often about a group of people, that has become fixed through time. A stereotype is usually wholly or partly untrue, and it is often used to negatively discuss people of a different race, ethnicity, religion, physical ability, or sexuality.

traumatic extremely unpleasant and causing great distress

FIND OUT MORE

Books

Amblard, Odile. *Friends Forever? Why Your Friendships Are So Important* (Sunscreen). New York: Amulet, 2008.

Cohn, Lisa, and Debbie Glasser. *The Step-Tween Survival Guide: How to Deal with Life in a Stepfamily*. Minneapolis: Free Spirit, 2008.

Hardyman, Robyn. *Relationships* (Being Healthy, Feeling Great). New York: PowerKids, 2010.

Hile, Lori. *Bullying* (Teen Issues). Chicago: Heinemann Library, 2013.

Hile, Lori. *Gangs* (Teen Issues). Chicago: Heinemann Library, 2013.

Mattern, Joanne. *Divorce* (Real Deal). Chicago: Heinemann Library, 2009.

Medina, Sarah. *Relationships* (Know the Facts). New York: Rosen, 2010.

Robinson, Matthew. *Making Smart Choices About Relationships* (Making Smart Choices). New York: Rosen, 2008.

Senker, Cath. *Self-Harm* (Teen Issues). Chicago: Heinemann Library, 2013.

Simons, Rae. *Blended Families* (Changing Face of Modern Families). Broomall, Pa.: Mason Crest, 2010.

Web sites

kidshealth.org/kid/feeling/home_family/blended.html
On this web site you can find advice about living with stepparents and their families.

kidshealth.org/teen/expert
Choose from links leading to discussions about a variety of topics discussed in this book.

kidshealth.org/teen/your_mind/relationships/abuse.html
Learn more about abusive relationships—and how to get out of them.

www.pbs.org/inthemix/bullying/
"Stop Bullying ... Take a Stand!" is a 30-minute documentary for teens about bullying, developed as part of an award-winning Public Broadcasting Service teen series.

www.stopbullying.gov
This government web site offers resources on bullying for kids, teens, parents, and educators, including webisodes about taking a stand on bullying, a list of warning signs, ways to get help, and information about cyberbullying.

www.teenhealthandwellness.com/static/hotlines
Use this web site to find help lines that are specific to a variety of issues mentioned in this book.

teenlineonline.org
If you are facing difficult issues in your life, you might want to talk to someone privately. Visit Teen Line online or call 800-852-8336. You can tell their advisors what is happening to you and they will give you help and advice. You can also look on the message boards to talk to other young people, so you will not feel so alone.

www.youngwomenshealth.org/healthy_relat.html
This web site is aimed at girls and includes information about healthy relationships with siblings, parents, and friends, as well as dating.

Topics to debate

- Think about the different relationships you have in your life. How are they different? Why are they different? Do you think you are the same person with everyone you know? If not, why not?

- Discuss your experiences with trust. Have there been times when you have trusted someone and been let down? Or have you let down someone who trusted you? Think of some ways to rebuild trust between individuals after a fight or disagreement.

- Why are boys expected to hide their emotions? Do you think this is a good thing or a bad thing? Have these expectations changed at all?

INDEX